A Childhood That Was Stolen
by the Prince of Darkness

A Childhood That Was Stolen by the Prince of Darkness

Lawrence Stinson

CITIOFBOOKS, INC.
3736 Eubank NE Suite A1
Albuquerque, NM 87111-3579
www.citiofbooks.com
Hotline: 1 (877) 389-2759
Fax: 1 (505) 930-7244

Ordering Information:
Quantity sales. Special discounts are available on quantity purchases by corporations, associations, and others. For details, contact the publisher at the address above.

Printed in the United States of America.

ISBN-13:   Softcover   979-8-89391-884-7
            eBook   979-8-89391-885-4

Library of Congress Control Number: 2025917715

My name is Lawrence Edward Stinson. I'm the author of this book. I was born in this little town called Holly Springs Mississippi to a woman by the name of Mrs. Lura Walton-Stinson. I am writing this book about childhood based on a true story. This is the heavenly truth which means I am not lying.

I remember when I was four years old, seeing my grandmother Ruby Pegues, my mother's momma, sitting outside under a big tree, it was a warm evening. She said my head is hurting and she started to crying and hollering so loud. All the grand children were outside praying. My grandmother's voice caught my attention. I was so frightened and scared that I stared and stared. One of the oldest grandchildren said "Go get mom some help, someone with a car." Back then black people did not have cars; well most of us didn't because of the poverty. A white man that my grandmother worked for did. We were very poor and less fortunate than some others. My grandmother was the mother of fourteen children. She had two sets of twins, my mother and uncle, Lura & Luther, a boy and a girl, and another set of twins, Eugene and Betty Jean another boy and girl twin. The white man that she worked for was Mr. Mack Peyton. He came back with my Aunt Marble Mc Neil and his mother. He told us that my grandmother had passed away with a heart attack. None of us grandchildren got to go to the funeral because we were too young to know about death or a funeral so I go over it.

At age 5, I went to a Head Start in Potts Camp Mississippi called Mary Reid. The first day I went to school I got a paddling in my hand. When I asked the teacher why, she said it was because I did not ask for permission to go to the bathroom. By the time I was in the second grade, I was thinking about girls, just like all of the other boys I knew. When I got to hird grade, my parents took all of us on a trip to Chicago. My father was unstable at times and would fight my mother a lot because he was jealous. I would stand in a corner crying loud to God asking Him to stop them. Our house wasn't in the best livable condition but there was a roof. We finally moved to Chicago and the first school I attended was Ben Baniker Elementary. We lived on 69th and Union Street. By the year of 1968 we had moved to 67th and Ellis Street. It was there that I remembered hearing the news of Martin Luther King being shot in Memphis at the Loraine Motel. We lived on the second floor of an apartment building and I could hear all of the vandalism of every store owned by a white man all night long. I didn't know anything about the Black Panthers, but I did know about the Black Stone Rangers and the Mighty Cobras at the age of 9. I heard them say "1, 2,3,4,5 the Black Stone Rangers don't take that jive." I looked outside of my window and saw them stomp a man so hard. So I went back to watch the late show of Elvis Presley on TV.

During my fourth grade year we traveled back to Mississippi. I had a teacher whose name I won't mention. She could really paddle if you messed up. My fifth grade teacher. He taught P.E. and was a basketball coach. My 6th grade year was integrated with black and whites together. My seventh grade teacher was Mrs. Betty Weathers, now Mrs. Betty Fountain and my eighth grade teacher was Mrs. Upshaw. In eighth grade at Potts Camp High School, I was a comedian and would make the whole class laugh all the time. You know it was still a lot of prejudice going on back then. One day in gym class I was marking my gym teacher on how he walked before he came back to class. He was a white man and was about 6ft tall. He was a stocky build. Everyone was laughing and someone said "here he comes Bozo". That was my nickname back then. I ran and sat down real quick, but everybody was still laughing really hard. Everybody was scared of him because he was so mean. He would paddle you or expel you if he thought something wasn't right. He asked in a nice way, "what are y' all laughing about" A little white girl, pointed me out. She had been doing that since the 6th grade. He said "come here boy, how do I walk?" I showed him he wasn't handicapped. He took me to the bathroom to clean every commode up. They were all nasty, full of feces, and stopped up with paper. I told him no so he told me to bend over and touch my toes. I said no again and he took me to the front office. The principle wanted to paddle me and I told him no too. He said he was going to tell my mother in a letter stating to let you go to a school that you like. He put in my records that I was kicked out of School. I got kicked out in the middle of my eighth grade year. I wanted to go to the Catholic School where all my relatives were, at Cadet, now called Holy Family. I went there first and one of the Sisters's told me to come back next year because it was so late in the year. She told me she was going to take this out of my records. She gave me the record and all the transcripts mailed to her so no other school got a chance to see my records. Thanks to her, I finished my 8th grade at Rosen Wall which is now Sims Intermediate and did my 9th grade year at Cadet High School. Mrs. Judy Autry was one of my teachers. I was going back and forth from Mississippi to Chicago to finish school. I would see people on TV making a living by being an actress or an entrepreneur. Mississippi did not have any drama classes and they still don't in 2013.

When I was young boy living with my parents, we were back and forth from Mississippi to Chicago. We lived with my uncle and aunt. At the age of 14 I was in the 10th grade, at 15 I was in the 11th grade, and at 16 I was in the 12th grade. In 1976 my graduation year, I had to go to night school for two extra credits. I had enough credits to graduate had I stayed in Mississippi. It took 18 units to graduate in the state of Illinois and 16 in Mississippi. In 1976 I will never forget the night Jessie Jackson was speaking on up with hope down with dope. I had to go to Chicago Vocational School to gain my two credits. I love to read the Holy Bible and my history book because I love black history. I made the highest score on my constitution test, 100 out of every one in the class. We couldn't study for the test and it was 1/3 of our grade. That night of Jessie Jackson's speech on my way home from high school, I left class on my way to the bus stop I was cold and it had just started to snow. I will never forget that night. I looked both ways and walked across the street between the white lines. I didn't know a car was speeding over the speed limit. I got hit and knocked up in the air with my feet in the air. When I came down my eyes were closed. When the care first hit me my eyes were opened and I saw my feet in the air while

I was in the air bottom side up. When I came down closing my eyes, hitting the ground, I felt something telling me to die, die, die. It was like a song. I finally opened my eyes and I was glad that I was not dead. I was looking up under a big Mack truck that had been rolling and stopped on dime. Touching my arm without damaging it, I thanked God. I remembered the paramedic pulled me inside of it. I had to have 168 stitches. Some of them were on the inside and some on the outside messing up a lot of leathers in my legs. After staying in the hospital for a while, I came home and couldn't walk for 9 months. I had to go to therapy to learn how to re-walk during my 9 months in bed. I read the Bible for the entire 9 months. It seems like something jumped out of the Bible into me. Something I couldn't see and no one else could see either. This was the house of my uncle and aunt. I wanted to go to church. My uncle fooled me and took me to a place called Tinley Park. There I stayed 9 months and during that time a strange incident happened to me. That night I didn't take my medication. I would fool the tenant like I took it when I actually hated taking that medicine. I hated that place. I ran up and down the hall tearing my shirt off whenever this thing would bother me. I came and told the tenant one night that someone was in my room. She came and looked and saw nothing. She told me to go back to my room and go to bed. She said if you don't to your room right now she was going to call the security guard and put me in lock down. I went back to my room and begin to fix my bed. I spread my sheet one time, it crumbled up. I spread it again and it crumbled up again. I was scared to go to the tenant because she was not going to believe me. I spread the sheet a third time and jumped on the bed and it crumbled up with me in it. It seemed like an earthquake was shaking up and down inside of me. I ran out in the hall jumping up and down telling the tenant something was inside of me. Then there was a big security guard weighing about 600 pounds caught me by the neck and threw me down to the floor on my back. He put his knee on my neck and I thought I was going to die. His knee was choking me to death. I couldn't holler or breathe. I pointed to my finger at neck and the lady tenant told him to move his knee from my neck so I could breathe. They put me in lock down and while I was in there I was in restraints. I could barley raise my arm to do the

Old Catholic way. I touched my tongue with my finger, my forehead in the center and my chest about 30 times or more. It was touched by the right way because it said you killed me.

After 9 months of Tinley Park, I see my mother's face. I was very happy because I knew I had someone on my side that would believe my story, listen to me, and comfort me. My mother and I were very close. She had come to get me to go back to Mississippi with her to take care of me. I heard the doctor say, "I heard you were coming back to get your son to take him back home with you". She replied "yes". The doctor said that he already had my transcript ready to be transferred to Jackson Mississippi. My uncle, aunt, and mother came to get me and took me back to 447 South Green Street to their house. My mother had caught a plane to take me back home. My uncle David lived in Chicago also. He took my mother and I to O'Hare airport. Somehow they would not let me ride the airplane, why? I don't know. You would have to ask my uncle because my mother is deceased now. My mother went back to the airport and bought a round trip ticket. She told my uncle David that she would do what he told her to do and get a car and drive back to pick me up. So we went back to 10447 South Green. I stayed there till my mother and father came to get me. We went back to Mississippi. I lived with my parents and two sisters, Annie and Vera Stinson back in Holly Springs. I didn't talk or speak in a whole year. I was in a state of shock and devastated about what happened to me in Tenley Park. I wonder how I could explain this to someone. When I got home in Mississippi I was quiet for a year. My people said "Bo won't talk unless we ask him a question, no conversation he would hold. We lived on Marianna Road in Holly Springs Mississippi. I started having heavenly dreams at night when I went to sleep. I remember all of them. Many of my dreams question me saying, "Do you drink and do you smoke?" First thing I thought about were cigarettes. Because I didn't smoke anything else, I just paused.

I started seeing the Bible scriptures and they were chapters and scriptures that I could quote. I also remember later before the year was over, by me not talking I closed my eyes to pray looking toward heaven at the same house. I did not want to live behind all of this drama. I did not want anyone to kill me in the streets. I just wanted God to take my life in my sleep on my prayer when I sleep. One night I prayed so hard, saying thank you Jesus at least a million times. What did I do that for? A voice called out my name. I could not hear myself pray or anything. The power of God raised everything in me. My vision was pointed towards heaven with my eyes closed. This is what a voice said to me as plain as it could be. It said "Lawrence, I been watching you. You be good down there." After that voice was no longer there, no picture of a face or nothing, my eyes came open. I knew it was the voice of Jesus Christ. The voice was plain and clear. It was like a strong commanding chief. I will not forget that great voice and I will also obey it. I did not tell anyone because; I knew they would not believe me. One day my father had taken my possessions and I was very angry. He had me sent back to the state hospital in Jackson Mississippi. There I stayed nine months, back in Holly Springs, and then back to Chicago. I went to Tenley Park on my own. Why? I wanted to investigate why they could not tell me what was wrong with me. I, Lawrence E. Stinson found out why. It was beyond my recognition and anyone else until this day, that I will prove it.

While I was in Tinley Park, I was doing my own investigation. That is the purpose that is why I went back to Chicago. At that time people were still there when I was a resident there, so I started to ask some of them some questions. They remembered me so I asked them about some of the strange things that happened to me at Timely Park. One guy said he remembered my, but he could not explain it to me. I stayed there three months. It was very funny and dangerous how I got back in Tinley Park. This is what happened. I did not let my uncle or aunt know that I was back in Chicago. I knew they would be afraid for me. They wanted me to stay in Mississippi for my own good. I came back to Chicago anyway. I lived in a shelter home downtown. The place was called "House of Christ". One morning early approximately 1:00am, I was sick and I was walking in every alley around my uncle and aunt's house, from 103rd street to 106th. I was checking every garage that it was until came upon this garage that was unlocked. I went into it searching for something to take. I could have been shot, but by the grace of God, I was not. I saw this lawn mower and took it. I was going to sell it when daylight came, but while I was pushing it up Halsted street, a police patrol car pulled up to the side of the street about 2:00am. They asked me where are you going, see I knew what I was doing, I was trying to get a way to Tinley Park. I said to them, I am on my way home, they said where is home, I said Tinley Park. So they loaded the lawn mower up in their trunk and put me in the back seat and off I went to Tinley Park.

Once I got back there, my investigation started. I stayed there for another three months. When I got out I went back to my uncle and aunt's house on 10447 S. Green Street. My uncle and aunt had five children, James Walton, Michael Walton, Renee Walton, Barbara Walton and Darryl Walton. They were like real brothers and sister. When my uncle found out that I was back in Chicago, he wanted me back in Mississippi immediately because he did not want me live with him anymore because of my illness. His brother-n-law, Mac Collins, was going to Mississippi to visit his relatives, so he asked him to take me back to Mississippi. So off I went back to my parent's house again in Mississippi.

When I slept at night, I would always have these dreams. I could remember all of them. Let me tell you about this one in particular, no one can tell you this story but me because it happened to me and me only and I could have died. Thanks to God that I am still alive.

On particular night I was at my Aunt Marable's house and I shared a bed with my cousin Willie Earl who is my first cousin. My aunt had a pretty large family and we had to share beds. Willie Earl slept on the back side of the bed and I slept on the front side. Every night before I go to bed, I would pray hard, that means a long time all night. I would close my eyes; know that, I am closing them seeking to see Jesus Christ's face. I was not asleep, but I had my eyes close not seeking to get a good night rest, but I was trying to find Jesus. So I began to say these words, "thank you Jesus, thank you Jesus, thank you Jesus". This continues on all night, every night. Every now and then I would out the corner of my eyes and close them. I could see shadows and they were very dark. I always wanted to see a shadow, not a dark shadow. So I kept praying to Jesus seeking an answer. I eased my eyes open and I saw a physical grim reaper standing up over my bed looking down at me. I did not know what that was at the time. I was very scared and I was afraid to close my eyes again. I kept my eyes open all night, I kept my fist balled up; because I was going to knock out if it touched me. I would rare back and it would jump back. I saw that it was afraid of me when I balled up my fist as well as I was afraid of it. I felt pretty good then, he I was communication through our mind. I would always do the talking to him in my mind. I was praying for Jesus and I knew that was not Jesus. So I played cards right, this is the way I looked at his face, it glowing white with no eyes and he had on a black hoodie, identical to a Sequin face. I told him, you are not Jesus. Jesus comes in threes, the Father, the Son, and the Holy Ghost. I would always be talking to in mind, not out loud. I told him you can touch me when Jesus Christ comes in threes. So he left and after a while he came back. My eyes were still open, I was determined that night not close my eyes until the day I die. He left and I kept on praying, then I looked at the wall and I saw a dancer. It was dancing, but it comforted my mind for the time being. But then here he comes again, but this time it was two more like him. I did not care about them. I kept my fist balled up. All three of them lined up by my bed. If I tried to move to another room, something in the other room would come and growl at my neck like it was going to bite it off. It sounded like some type of animal, beside the three of them. But as long as I didn't want to get up, it would go back in the other room and make strange noises. Seem like it knew when I was going to get up. I was very, very scared of that thing. But back to the three evil spirits, the first one wanted to touch me and the other two on my hip. I drew back my fist again and said, "I will knock you out, all three of you, if you tough me!" if they would touched me, I believe I would have died. I told them if Jesus comes in fours then you can touch me. I was trying to wait on day light. They came back once again this time in fives. They lined up and down my bed, bit I busted their bubble and said Jesus comes in white and they were dressed in black with white faces. They were astonishing and about this time, it was 4:59am, one minute before the break of daylight. They started to evaporate away, one at a time. A little crack was in the back of the door were we slept that lead to the outside. Finally it was daylight, I was glad and I looked at the door and said how this could be. I didn't tell anyone about this dream until now, because it would have scared them.

The next thing I did was keep it to myself. I did not want to scare anyone, so went on like nothing ever happened. Around this time, I had a lawsuit in about a car wreck. The lawyer wrote me at my mother's address. The letter stated that he had my case settled. To be honest, I had completely forgotten about the lawsuit. The letter said the settlement was for $24,000 and I would receive about $12,000. I had even forgotten about my education when I was in night school. I had started to deal people again and I tried to get into Rust College, I said yeah! Rust College sent for my records but the report came back saying I had 171/2 credits. That did not please me. The admission clerk to enter into college at Rust College in Holly Springs Mississippi. I thought to myself, they know darn well I finished high school. So I called Percy Julian High School in Chicago Illinois and one of the staff members looked up my records and said I am sorry to say you were not promoted. I was very angry, but by the time I had so much stress on me, I was sent back to Jackson Mississippi hospital again.

It was around 1982 and everyone had heard my $12,000 was coming in soon and again I had forgotten about school. A guy who I thought was very close to me, who likes to gamble a lot and he never went to church, started riding with me everywhere he went. He knew my money was coming so when I did get my money, he and his wife took me straight to the bank. He and his wife to be the overseer of my money but the banker told me you don't need any one over your money, it stands s for itself. Just you alone will be fine. But he and his wife said, "Bo needs a guardian over that money. He might mess it all up." So I decided to put her name on my account. They told me "Bo, you don't have to worry about anything anymore."

To this day I regret that decision to put his wife on my account because they took everything that I had. I went off like a light bulb, I wanted to kill them both, but I was sent back to Jackson Mississippi State Hospital. I hated every minute of it. While I was sent back and forth Jackson Mississippi State Hospital, I thought about my school education. When I got out again, I went back to Chicago to question Percy Julian High School about my diploma. It was a simple problem but I had the straighten it out. One of my teachers forgot to put the other ½ credit on my report card, but by this time all of my teachers were gone, retired, or deceased. Then they told me you are to come back to high school to get a ½ credit. So what was I going to do now? I was so frustrated and found myself back at Tinley Park. I was getting older. I had been in Tinley Park off and on. When I got out Tinley Park this last time, I went back to Holly Springs and found myself back at the Jackson Mississippi State Hospital.

The last time I got out of the Mississippi State Hospital, I thought about my education again. I called the Chicago Board of records, where they keep school records. I kept calling to finally I got someone to help me. I explained to this lady how many times I had been to Chicago for this matter. She said I remember that class you took carries as a double class. I finally got my diploma! I did not have enough credits to go to the university; I had to go to a community college. I went there for about a year. The community college was called Northwest Mississippi Jr. College. Unfortunately by now I was older and my eyesight had failed me. I couldn't see like I wanted too. I passed philosophy but failed music. I didn't go back to Rust College. I was 51 years old, but I went blind in one of my eyes when I was in Tinley Park.

I had a hard time in life and God had delivered me. Now I am in church preaching the gospel. I found out not to hate and to love. I forgave that couple that took my money. I own nothing in this world and I will take nothing out. I now have a closer understanding with Christ Jesus. I am also married to the love of my wife, Brenda Rooks Stinson. We have three children, Breneta Clark, Lawndra Stinson and LaDarius Stinson. In addition, I have one deceased precious angel, Lil Miss Nyesha Lanett Stinson. My daughter has two boys, my grandsons Kaleb and Kylen Boyd. They are not twins they just have twin names.

About the Author

I live in a small town called Holly Springs, MS. I am now married to my supportive Wife Belinda Rooks-Stinson. With this union we have 3 children Breneta, lawndrea and Ladarius. We also have 3 grandchildren. I am writing this story because I survived, I survived an evil spirit who has over taken many lives before mine. Christ the Savior was by my side helping me overcome these horrific tragedies. I wrote this book to get my word out and to help others going through troubled times.